<u>Agile</u>
<u>&</u>
<u>Quality by Design</u>

Ronald N. Goulden, MBA, PMP

Agile & Quality by Design

Copyright © 2015

Ronald N. Goulden, MBA, PMP

ALL RIGHTS RESERVED

Cover design by Ronald Goulden

ISBN: 978-1512132588

Table of Contents

Introduction

Originally, projects were managed by a process that could be called the Monolithic Project Delivery (MPD) methodology, where the senior IT leadership gathered preliminary requirements from the customer and then sequestered the team until the project was designed and completed; which in many cases took years.

Typically, when the project was delivered under this methodology, it did not meet the needs of the user and. in fact the sponsor may have moved on, resulting in a costly 'orphaned' project that no one particularly wanted or understood. Additionally, this methodology captured a static set of requirements in what was very likely an environment of constantly evolving needs, resulting in a product that was obsolete before it was even delivered.

Over the years, project delivery methodologies improved to provide milestones and incremental deliverables with associated deadlines. However, milestones slipped regularly and most projects under-delivered and over-spent, both in time, money, and quality. In fact, quality was often sacrificed in the rush to meet the time or cost delivery requirements; resulting in a sub-standard or a completely unusable product.

In an attempt to solve these problems, the Agile methodology was developed and has gained widespread acceptance. However Agile focuses on functionality instead of quality.

Agile is not new. Many years ago, project leaders began working closely with the user community and engaged them throughout the entire project process.

This ensured that the users were involved in determining what they wanted and how it would be presented. Through this natural course of human involvement, the requirements evolved naturally to meet the needs of the customers, ensuring greater satisfaction with the results. By engaging the user, the development team ensured that they delivered to meet the needs of the user and also gained incremental user 'ownership' of the product.

The underlying principle was to place the needs of the customer first. Sometimes, this is referred to as Extreme Programming, or XP. This concept places customer satisfaction first by providing the functions and features the customer wants, rather than what the developer wants to deliver. Typically, this provides a rapid response to dynamic customer demands and encompasses Continuous Integration (CI), which involves frequent changes to the code, and subsequently frequent code delivery.

Another important function to consider is code refactoring. This involves integrating small changes to the look and feel of the project continuously, over time. Refactoring is not a bug or defect and should not be treated as such. It is merely an aspect of continuous improvement and evolution, and is ideally suited for an Agile environment.

In 2001, Agile was officially born, though as I have already mentioned, it had actually been in use by many technology departments long before then; it just had not been formalized or named.

The fact that the Quality Assurance (QA) function is typically compartmentalized away from the development function also aggravates quality issues. Too often, there is an invisible 'fence' between the development and quality teams which inhibits teamwork and often promotes an antagonistic relationship between the two groups.

Isolation of the development and quality teams results in a fragmented effort and sub-standard results. Development rushes to meet a deadline, and quality often has little or no understanding of the user requirements. It is not uncommon for a Quality Assurance team to completely redesign an application after it has been developed and delivered to them for testing.

This is where Quality by Design can be quite effective by requiring that the development teams are responsible for quality and the quality teams are responsible for understanding the user requirements by being fully engaged in the project from the outset rather than at the end.

From a business perspective, there is great value to be gained from Agile methodologies. The business can respond more rapidly to the needs of its customers or internal and external demands. However, since Agile focuses on functionality over quality, the developers must take ownership of their efforts, and be responsible for quality through the entire development lifecycle.

Overview - What is Agile?

What is Agile? If you go to a browser and search for "What is Agile", you will get results that talk about 'scrum', 'adaptability', 'iterative delivery' etc.

In the most simplistic of terms, Agile is a project management methodology that focuses on short development cycles, called sprints, wherein small tasks, or stories, are delivered to the customer on a regular basis.

This is at extreme variance with the Monolithic Project Delivery (MPD) methodology. Agile differs from the traditional project management methodologies such as waterfall, spiral, Six Sigma, and any number of variants and hybridizations in that the development cycle is often very short.

Agile is a methodology focused on rapidly providing deliverables and actively engaging the customer throughout the development process. Part of Agile's strength is its valuation of individuals, communication and collaboration among the team members and its ability to quickly respond to changing user requirements, hence its name, Agile. For the most part Agile and Scrum will be used interchangeably.

There are four primary components to the Agile Scrum Framework:
1. The three primary Agile roles:
    a. Product Owner
    b. Scrum Master
    c. Scrum Team Members
2. A Prioritized backlog of work requests.
3. The Sprints
4. Scrum Events (meetings)

With Agile, there are three basic roles; Product Owner, Scrum Master, and Scrum Team Member. Any team member can perform a variety of functions. A team typically consists of up eight or ten people, depending on the needs of the business.

There are no specialized roles such as Project Manager, Tester, developer, DBA, etc. There are only Product Owner, Scrum Master, and Scrum Team Member. All team members are treated as equals, regardless of their function.

The Product Owner is the Primary stakeholder, or Sponsor in a typical Project Management environment.

As with any project management methodology, the Product Owner (Sponsor) is the one who is authorized to allocate funding for the project and its related sprints.

Again, stakeholders are those people, teams, and groups who have an interest in or may be impacted by the development efforts.

Every business environment has a list of projects that it wants worked. In Agile, this list is called the Backlog. Ideally, every story in the backlog will be prioritized by the Product Owner(s) so that they can easily be scheduled into sprints for development. In reality, the Backlog may grow faster than the Product Owners can prioritize them and this may require multiple passes before they properly prioritize the entire Backlog.

Due to the need for great responsiveness and agility, work is divided into work efforts called Sprints. A sprint can be as little as two weeks and up to several weeks, depending upon the needs of the business and the development environment.

An important aspect of Agile is that each feature, or micro-project, is represented as a story. Each story must be completed and tested before moving to the next story or feature in the sprint.

If you have a tester role on the scrum team, that means that the developer completes a story and turns it over to the tester as soon as it is ready, then begins work on the next story or feature (being aware that if defects are discovered in the original story deliverable, the developer must correct the defects and return to the tester).

In the Quality by Design model, the developer tests thoroughly while developing, then has a team member perform a code review and secondary testing before allowing the story to progress to the tester.

Over the course of a sprint, there are several necessary meetings, called Scrum Events that have to occur. These meeting include, but are not limited to:

1. Backlog Prioritization meetings
2. A Sprint Planning meeting
3. Daily Scrum Stand-up meeting
4. A Sprint Review meeting
5. A Sprint Retrospective Meeting

A critical success factor for Agile is active involvement and communication among the team and with the Product Owner.

The preliminary requirements are high level with the expectation that more detail will evolve over the course of the sprint.

The focus is to provide small, incremental improvements rather than large, all-encompassing releases. It is far better to deliver most of what a user wants as quickly as possible than to postpone delivery until the story is perfect (which is impossible).

Two points to be wary of are scope creep and gold-plating. Scope creep comes from the business while gold-plating is caused by the developers and testers.

Due to the responsive nature of Agile, it is a seductive environment for the Product Owner and other business leaders to want to add 'fly-by' requests that materially affect the ability of the team to deliver on its sprint commitments.

The Scrum Master and team members must be able to 'push-back' and communicate with the Product Owner that new features have to deduct from what can be delivered within the sprint. Typically, sprint resources are closely monitored and tightly scheduled. A change of even just a few hours can result in a failed sprint.

The most insidious threat to sprint deliverables is called 'gold-plating'. This occurs when a developer adds unrequested and undocumented features to the story. (Often, a developer will try a new programming technique or add a new capability that should only take a few minutes; but in reality, consumes large amounts of development time.) The testing function can also contribute to gold-plating by insisting that additional features be added. This is why the definition of done and acceptance criteria are so important and must be clearly documented and communicated to all parties.

'Gold-plating' and scope creep are the causes of many failed projects. Often these changes are subtle and seem so innocuous that the temptation is to 'go ahead and include them'. But these 'little' changes quickly add up and can consume all available time and effort, resulting in the original goal of the story being neglected and not delivered.

Agile Manifesto

Some basic Agile concepts are:
1. Processes are not as important as the individual team members and their interactions.
2. Tools do **not** take priority over the individual.

3. The team should spend their time producing a working solution rather than convoluted documentation.
4. Collaborate with the customer rather than contract with them.
5. Always be willing to embrace change rather than try to adhere to a documented plan.

There are twelve published Agile principles that form the Agile Manifesto and the formal document can be found on the Internet.

A brief summary of the manifesto follows:
1. Customer Satisfaction comes first.
2. Always welcome change.
3. Deliver changes as frequently as possible.
4. The business and developers work as a team.
5. Have a motivated team
6. Use face-to-face communication when possible, rather than email or phone.
7. Deliver functionality.
8. Find a delivery pace that can be sustained.
9. Have attention to good design.
10. Keep It Simple.
11. Self-organized teams can produce superior designs.
12. Self-reflection.

The Agile team should always focus on deliverables over documentation. However, that does not imply there is no documentation. Design documents such as IPO charts are critical success factors to ensure that the team delivers what the business is asking for. Lack of design documentation will result in chaos and failure.

Again, flexibility is also important. Do not groom a sprint and assume it is 'locked in' and that there will be no changes. There is always change.

Agile provides for Continuous Integration (CI) and Continuous Deployment (CD), though this capability may be unfeasible in some environments due to existing bureaucratic change control processes.

Continuous Integration is a concept of constantly changing the code and environment to meet ever-changing demands of the business and to consistently keep up with the dynamically changing needs of the business.

Continuous Deployment involves the deployment of any successfully tested and built story into the production environment as quickly as possible, in order to provide a constant flow of deliverables to the customer. The upside of this is that the business perceives a development environment that is constantly providing value to the business, rather than having to wait until the end of the sprint.

Be aware that Continuous Integration and Continuous Delivery may not work in all environments.

Agile will face challenges if the development team is using scrum techniques while the remainder of the business is locked into monolithic practices and processes. If there are lengthy or convoluted approval processes in place, the act of deploying new code may take as much time as it took the team to develop the code itself. If a business plans to use Agile, all aspects of the development and deployment processes must be reviewed and revised as necessary to allow the business to reap the benefits of rapid development.

Overview - What is Quality by Design?

Quality by Design is a concept that uses iterative development and test cycles to ensure that the application evolves and passes through several layers of testing before delivery to the customer.

Quality by Design is a formalized, documented process whereby each phase of testing is documented and errors and flaws are recorded, counted, and graphed.

Again, this concept was developed to resolve the 'toss it over the fence' relationship that often existed between Development staff and Quality Assurance (QA).

Historically, the developer would write code and 'test' it, then hand it off to the QA team, who would subject it to a more rigorous test process, invariably discovering some issues which were returned to the developer for resolution. This cycle often became drawn out and contentious, especially if the QA team used the 'test until break' concept where testing stops at the first defect and is returned to the developer. This is an inefficient and counter-productive test methodology that is intended to be punitive.

Another historical problem was that in some cases, the QA department would 'redesign' the application at the end of the process because 'they knew what the customer needs'. Again, this led to a contentious and wasteful redevelopment cycle, delaying the project delivery even more.

Quality by Design focuses on multiple test points within four key quality areas within the development process; Development Testing (D), Operational testing (O), Procedural Testing (P), and Integration testing (I). These four test functions are to be performed by the development team and requires careful recording of issues and errors as part of a 'lessons learned' exercise.

Once the development team thoroughly tests the application, it can be delivered to the QA team with reasonable confidence that the application functions as expected.

The QA team is expected to follow the same test methodology (DOPI) along with other standardized testing processes. As with the developers, their results are recorded as well. A special spreadsheet, called the Quality Scorecard is used for recording defects and issues and can graphically illustrate the effectiveness and progress of quality through the application lifecycle.

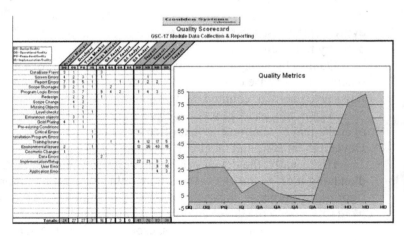

Figure 1 Quality Scorecard

8

Historically, the Quality Lifecycle is much like the example in Figure 1. Note that the development errors and defects tend to 'flat line', and then decline rapidly before delivering to QA. In QA, there is typically a spike in defects or issues which ultimately decline to near zero. However, upon delivery to the customer, there is historically a huge increase in defects and issues; some are related to development and some are related to other influences such as environmental, training, implementation, operations, etc.

Using the Quality Scorecard, project managers can quickly identify recurring 'pain points' in the development-quality lifecycle and apply lessons learned concepts to continuously improve overall quality processes.

Besides the traditional testing environment like code reviews, Systems Integration Testing (SIT), Customer Acceptance Testing (CAT), Pre-Prod, and Post-Prod, Design by Quality installs four additional development cycle metrics:

- **DQ - D**esign **Q**uality

During the early stages of development, the developer will discover environmental and design issues that may have been overlooked in the initial planning stages. These are defects that need to be addressed, logged, and reported. This may include data sources that are incorrect, improperly defined, or not functional.

- **OQ - O**perational **Q**uality

Once the design issues are resolved and recorded, the developer can begin on the actual coding and functional testing of the story. The reportable criteria here would be issues that prevent the code from functioning as expected, not specific coding issues. It may be as simple as needing to use a different version of a function call or redesign of a web service call.

During this phase, it is wise to have a second developer do a quick code review and independent test to ensure that the obvious has not been overlooked. (Developers will test using a specific routine which always works for them; a second developer may try a different approach that brings to light coding flaws.)

- **PQ - P**rocedural **Q**uality

Once the individual code segment works as expected, the developer performs procedural testing wherein it is determined if the code 'plays nicely' with

9

other segments of code. This is a form or integration testing. Any issues that arise must be recorded.

Often this will identify areas where independent segments of code must be adjusted to ensure that they work correctly with each other. Sometimes this may be as simple as how date strings are formatted. (Code segment A may use a mm-dd-yyyy format while code segment B uses a dd-mm-yy format.)

- **IQ - Implementation Quality**

The final stage of development testing is the implementation stage. In this phase, the developers ensure that the installation scripts, packages, and documentation are in order and function correctly. Any problems, issues, and flaws must be recorded.

Ideally, at this point, the developer has communicated with the downstream implementers to ensure that all information and work instructions are accurate and meet the needs of the implementation teams. Some things to be considered are if processes have to be stopped and restarted, is there a specific time frame that the code needs to be implemented, and an estimate of how long the implementation process should take.

Design by Quality is not intended to be a punitive tool, but a learning mechanism. By accurately accounting for and recording all issues during the development cycle, the developers and designers can be aware of historical problems and take steps to avoid them, improving performance and productivity in subsequent sprints.

Only when the four development test metrics are fulfilled can the code move to the next phase.

Code Review

Once the developer is confident that the code is correct and fully tested, it needs to go through a code review. This is peer-review of the code and scripts and includes developers and implementers.

During this review, suggestions for improvements may be provided that will improve efficiencies and streamline the implementation process. Any suggestions made during the code review must be strongly considered, possibly enforced by management.

This is an ideal time for the developer and the implementers to discuss and document any requirements for implementation such as processes needing to be shut down and restarted, any specific implementation windows, and an estimate of how long the implementation process should take.

Testing

Different organizations have different levels of test environments. Some may have up to seven or eight levels of testing before an application can be implemented into production.

For the sake of brevity, this discussion will focus on the three most common; Systems Integration Testing (SIT), Customer Acceptance Testing (CAT), and Pre-Production (Pre-PROD).

Each testing level looks for specific issues and capabilities, with each subsequent test environment becoming more stringent. Regression testing is an important part of the QA cycle and should be included with increasing rigidity at each level of the testing cycles, ensuring ever increasing levels of quality controls.

Under no circumstance should a 'Test until Break' mentality be employed. (This is a punitive mindset sometimes taken by QA teams where they stop testing as soon as a defect is discovered and turn the story back to the developers. This results in a frustrating and wasteful cycle of detecting and correcting a long series of small issues rather than correcting many issues at one time. <u>The full test plan must be executed, noting ALL flaws and defects</u>.

System Integration Testing

When a story or application has passed code review, it is delivered to the team of testers, or Quality Assurance (QA). During this phase, the QA team determines if there are fundamental flaws or short-falls in the application itself.

Using test steps provided by the development team, the QA team should record and report any flaws and return the code to the developers for correction only after the entire test plan has been executed. Additionally, the QA team may use standard test routines that have been developed and used in the past to identify any unexpected results.

Note: the QA team should test the application completely before returning the code to the developers for correction. It is imperative that the QA team does not engage in the 'test until break' methodology, where as soon as a flaw of defect is detected, the code is returned to the developer. This is a very wasteful and counter-productive practice.

Customer Acceptance Testing

Once the code has been thoroughly and successfully tested in the SIT environment and it has management approval to promote to the next environment, the QA team can begin Customer Acceptance Testing.

This is a more intense and detailed testing process where all aspects of the code are tested, and included regression testing.

Again, this is a continuous testing process where all defects and flaws are recorded and accumulated before returning to the developer for any corrections.

Typically, after passing this test level, the Product Owner should review the results and compare them with the documented acceptance criteria. If there are discrepancies between the results and the acceptance criteria, the Product Owner makes the determination if the story is rejected or advanced with the exceptions noted.

Pre-Production Testing

After passing CAT testing, the application is reviewed by a different QA team to perform a final 'sanity check' to ensure that nothing has been missed or that there are any glaring flaws or omissions.

If the Pre-PROD environment is a mirror of the Production environment, final acceptance and approval at this stage should ensure a successful production implementation.

Much of the testing being performed at this stage will be regression testing to ensure that the new features work as expected in an environment that mirror5s the Production environment, while not 'breaking' any existing feature or capability.

While there may be a tendency to rush through this phase, since the code has already been tested intensively and the customer has accepted it, the QA team must proceed cautiously because there may be subtle variances between the lower environments and the Production environment that will allow fully tested code to fail when moved to Production. (It is not uncommon for extensively tested and validated code to fail when it is moved into Production. This may be a result of slight variations in the Production environment that are not mirrored in the lower environments. Any such discrepancies must be documented on the Quality Scorecard and addressed as quickly as possible.)

Post-Production Testing

Finally, once the code has been deployed to production, the developers and again, the QA team must perform regression testing on the live product to ensure the new code has not caused older code to fail.

Any defects found during Post-Production must be brought to the attention of management and resolved as quickly as possible.

As with all other levels of the Quality by Design process, any defects must be recorded and reported.

One additional function of the Quality by Design Post-Production process is to monitor the application or system through the 'warranty' period, which is typically thirty days. Any issues that arise during this time-frame must be recorded as well.

Typically, issues discovered during the Post-Production phase will be related to installation, environment, training, and documentation.

Using the Quality Scorecard to monitor Post-Production defects and flaws provides an excellent forum for addressing any inconsistencies between the Production environment and the lower environments, thus offering an opportunity for continuous improvement.

Many companies will merely acknowledge that the lower levels are not compatible with Production and plan to fix defects as they occur. This results in wasted effort and consumes development time in subsequent sprints. In the long run, it is best to correct any deficiency in the environments as quickly as possible to avoid unnecessary rework and dissatisfaction.

Why Combine Agile with Quality by Design?

As has been previously mentioned, Agile provides for a very fast development & delivery capability. However, since Agile focuses on functionality over quality, this speed of delivery often comes at the price of quality.

There are times that the Agile pace is so frenetic that the developers focus entirely upon delivering stories (features). This is often the fault of the Scrum Master, though the Agile coach and Product Owners have to share responsibility for this as well.

Quality is highly at risk for short sprints of less than three weeks. A two-week sprint can be quickly consumed by Scrum events (meetings), normal business, and 'fly-by' requests. (Remember that no one ever works at 100% of capacity; there are always distractions.)

On short sprint cycles, it is imperative that the Scrum events and meetings be kept as efficient as possible. If an eight member scrum team is involved for an hour each for: a Sprint Planning meeting, a Sprint Review meeting, a Sprint Retrospective Meeting, and ten fifteen-minute daily Scrum Stand-up meetings, there is the potential to lose more than twenty-six hours out of the development time form each sprint. (This does not take into consideration, phone calls, breaks, subject Matter expert questioning, etc.)

When the delivery focuses on functionality over quality, there is a significant risk of defects, rework, and re-design; all of which will detract from the performance of subsequent sprint. If the first half of each sprint is used to correct defects and quality issues, the effectiveness of Agile is greatly diminished.

Quality by Design is a tool that provides an incremental approach to improving deliverables' quality in a fashion that closely parallels the sprint cycle and the Agile methodology.

At the end of each sprint, during the retrospective meeting, the team can review the Quality Scorecard and identify areas where they can improve and where they can help teams outside of the scrum to improve by identifying flaws in training, documentation, implementation, timing, and even environmental short-comings.

I recommend that the implementation teams be included in the retrospective meeting because they can help identify ways for the development team to optimize their install scripts and processes.

By using open communications, the Agile process can be greatly enhanced and business satisfaction will grow.

Agile Concepts

Scrum Personalities

The Agile/scrum environment consists of multiple personalities. Typically, there will be the Product Owner, the Scrum Master, the Scrum Team Members, and possibly an Agile coach.

While each personality has specific functions and responsibilities, there are no solid role definitions. Each team member helps and learns whenever possible.

Unlike traditional development and Project Management environments, Agile does not have job description such as programmer, analyst, project manager, etc. This allows for seamless integration of efforts and promotes cross-training among the team members.

Product Owner

The Product Owner is typically the primary stakeholder and often fills the role of Sponsor in traditional Project Management methodologies. As a sponsor, the Product Owner represents the business and its stakeholders and makes sure the right work is being done at the proper time.

Remember that the Product Owner is the person who can commit business funding to projects and stories. Therefore, the Product Owner must be responsible for the backlog and what is included in each sprint.

The Product Owner and Scrum Master must work closely with each other and the Scrum team. Only the Product Owner can determine tasks and priorities.

With respect to release management, the Product Owner determines what stories are acceptable and with what level of functionality, both factors impact the costs associated with the Sprint.

The Product Owner should act as a buffer between business management and the Scrum team. Requirements, functionality, and acceptance criteria should be collected and merged into coherent stories that can be completed during a sprint and either added to the backlog as a future effort or assigned to a sprint.

As part of the Scrum environment, the Product Owner must work closely with the Scrum Master and the Scrum team members to ensure that everyone understands the requirements. Ultimately, the Product Owner must approve completed stories for promotion into a production environment.

The Product Owner maintains the backlog, the prioritized list of stories, and can answer most questions, or work with the team and stakeholders to provide answers as necessary.

Again, the Product Owner is responsible for managing the backlog, determining what is released for production, and managing the expectation of the business management teams.

Some of the Product Owner functions include:
- Goal-setting for the team
- Provides strategic and tactical planning for the team
- Shares status and communicates the team's deliverables with stakeholders
- Determines release dates for each sprint
- Determines requirements and acceptance criteria

Scrum Master

The Scrum Master can be viewed as the Project Manager/Administrative Assistant for the team. This role also functions as the Agile 'enforcer', ensuring that the agreed upon Scrum rules and practices are maintained.

The Scrum Master may wear many hats and perform many ancillary functions for the Scrum team. The Scrum Master works with the team to assign stories to team members.

In some environments, the Scrum Master is determined by the Scrum team, though in many cases, the role is assigned by business management.

Typically, the Scrum Master will have no administrative or line management responsibilities for the team members. This enables and promotes open communication. In the event of administrative issues, the Scrum Master may act as an advocate in discussions with line management, or the Product Owner.

The Scrum Master acts as a gatekeeper, to minimize external influences on the team. In many instances, the Scrum Master assumes the role of impediment resolver; either directly solving those issues or managing the attentions of those who can clear the impediments.

One of the most common functions of the Scrum Master is to control 'urgent', 'fly-by' requests from the business. The Scrum Master works with the Product Owner to negotiate these requests; either moving them to the backlog, or determining which current sprint stories will be sacrificed for the new request.

The Scrum Master is the facilitator and 'Master of Ceremonies' for the various Scrum events, such as the daily stand-up meeting, along with the Sprint planning, review, and retrospective meetings

Scrum Team Members

The Scrum Team Members are those actually committing to the work and deliverables. They can be developers, business analysts, data base administrators, network administrators, or virtually any other functional role necessary to fulfill the commitments. (In Scrum, titles are meaningless. All team members are equal, without any managerial hierarchy.)

Scrum team members perform all functions of a traditional project, such as: analysis, design, coding, and testing. The skillsets of the team members may vary dramatically; some may only be able to perform a few functions, while some may perform all functions.

The efforts of the sprint should focus on providing business value. If Scrum team members are working on intangible tasks that provide no direct benefit or functional value to the business, they are not following Agile concepts. Be wary of having too many 'research' stories in a sprint. The maximum should be one or two, depending on the size of the team.

The Scrum Master and Product Owner should focus on keeping Scrum Team Members out of meetings that have no direct effect on the developers' work. That being said, there are instances where the team members act as Subject Matter Experts (SMEs) and can provide valuable contributions to planning and design sessions for future deliverables or can benefit directly by participating in these meetings.

There is always some argument about documentation; many feel that the Scrum Team Members should not be involved in packaging releases, providing supporting documents and functions for release management, and should not be engaged in audit and source control processes. However, these are actually fundamental functions of any development activity and must be considered a part of the development process within the Sprint.

Typically, Scrum teams are relatively small, from six to ten members with varying skill sets. Each team member is equal in political stature to others; again, there is no hierarchy in Scrum Teams beyond Product Owner and Scrum Master.

Ideally, the Scrum team members are collocated and assigned full-time to the team. For the most part, the Scrum teams are self-managing and fully accountable for Sprint deliveries. This means that if the team commits to delivering a story in a sprint, they must honor that commitment and work extra hours if necessary to complete the story on time.

The Scrum team must define their rules and processes, such as the time and place of the daily stand-up meetings, definitions of ready and done, and consequences for violating the rules.

Working with the Product Owner and the Scrum Master, the Scrum team defines what it will commit to delivering, and task breakdown and assignments. (Remember that commitments must be honored, because management will often report expectations to their managers. A critical Agile skill is managing expectations.

The Scrum team members have the ability to 'push back' on a story assignment. However, the reality is that the Scrum team must provide value to the business. (Be aware that if the Team 'pushes back' on a business essential story, the Product Owner can simply move all stories to the backlog and only authorize the requested story to be worked on.)

While empowerment is a tremendous benefit, abuse of that empowerment will dismantle Agile efforts. If a Scrum team is not providing verifiable, functional benefits to the business, the team is failing its mission.

The Scrum team is responsible for reviewing the stories and dissecting them into achievable, verifiable tasks. The team is also responsible for accurately managing and reporting their daily time and efforts for the Sprint so that the Scrum Master can adequately report Sprint progress to the Product Owner and upper management.

As with any new team, maximum efficiency and performance is not achieved immediately. Any team will follow the Tuckman model of forming, storming, norming, and performing. How long that takes varies for every team. Typically, a Scrum team becomes effective after three or four sprints.

Tuckman Model of group Development

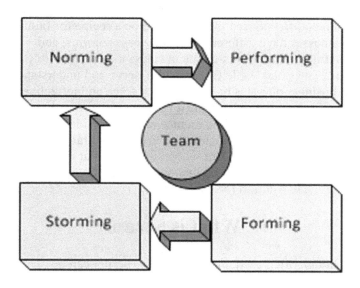

Agile Coach

The Agile Coach is an individual experienced with the Agile methodology and can help guide the Product Owner, Scrum Master, and Scrum Team Members to the greater efficiencies to be garnered with Agile. (The Coach should be viewed as a consultant and not an actual member of the team or the Scrum Framework.)

Be aware that the Agile Coach must not have any line management responsibilities for the stories of the Scrum team members. In no way should the coach be considered as part of the chain of command.

The purpose of the Coach is to mentor new Scrum teams, Scrum Masters, and Product Owners in the concepts of the Agile methodologies. The Agile Coach's scope of responsibility must not include disciplinary capabilities.

There are instances where the Agile coach must approach upper management to recommend changes to internal business processes. This is often the case if there are cumbersome approval and code promotion processes in place that seriously degrade sprint performance.

In some cases, the Agile Coach may attempt to fit a textbook or prior Agile experience into a new business environment. Be advised that this could be a recipe for failure. All businesses have different rules, processes, norms, and personalities. What works in one business may fail horribly in the next. The smart Agile Coach will observe and understand the way a business operates before trying to force an ineffective process. <u>By its nature, Agile must be adaptive.</u>

It is advantageous if the mentor is from outside the organization, with no political affiliations or aspirations. However, care must be taken with consultants that may focus more on extending a contract than in implementing the best possible Agile solution for the business.

What is Scrum?

Though often used interchangeably, Scrum can be considered to be a sub-set of the Agile methodology.

As previously mentioned, project requirements change frequently, causing chaos and failure in a typical software development environment. Unless the development team has extraordinary management, a conventional development environment will collapse under the weight of never-ending request for changes.

This is where Agile, and most specifically, Scrum, takes an incremental approach to software development, providing small, discrete, and useable components to fulfill the needs of the customer. Due to the short duration of the sprints, new features can be quickly accommodated without any devastating impact on schedules.

The scrum team works with great flexibility to meet the needs of the customer. For the most part, they are self-managing and are typically co-located so that questions and issues are resolved quickly without the latency of phone calls, email, or meetings.

The daily stand-up meeting is a 'safe' forum in which each team member may explain what was accomplished the previous day, what is expected to be accomplished for the current day, and iterates any impediments or obstacles perceived. (Management or other team members are expected to resolve those impediments.)

Another scrum concept is acceptance that the full scope of the problem may not be known or understood and that a detailed design effort is not required. The team only needs to know what is necessary to fulfill the needs of the particular story. (Hence, the caution about gold-plating.) The story should only solve a specific issue, not potential or future issues.

The difference between Scrum & Traditional Project Management

Traditional Project Management focuses on the traditional triangle of Cost – Time – Quality. While these are realistic metrics for longer term project management methodologies, this combination may be irrelevant for the much shorter Sprint methodology.

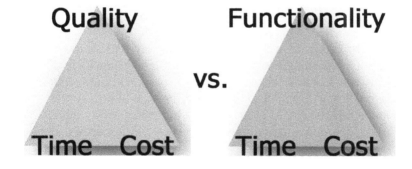

Scrum focuses more on Cost – Time – Functionality. While popular references will boldly state that quality is not a requirement for Scrum and is therefore much better than traditional project management, I disagree.

The frenetic pace of most Sprints tends to leave a gaping hole with respect to quality. Often, sub-standard results can be injected into Production environments because quality takes a backseat to functionality. Thus, the reason for this book.

It is quite possible to deliver stories that meet all of the acceptance criteria and still not function properly, resulting in production defects, which in most businesses, must be addressed as a critical defect. A production system that does not function properly has no value to the business and detracts from the credibility of the development team and Agile.

Realistically, the Scrum triangle must be Cost – Time – Quality/Functionality. Quality and Functionality is the ONLY option. Providing functionality that breaks the production system or performs poorly is not acceptable. It is incumbent upon the developer to thoroughly test the story during all phases of the development cycle, BEFORE releasing it to the Quality Assurance team. Remember, the question the Scrum Master and the Scrum team must ask is; "**Do you want it right, or do you want it right now?**"

Too often scrum teams see fast sprints as an opportunity to dodge rules and the need for quality, and to neglect documentation.

Remember that it is human nature to work up until a deadline before delivering a product. This results in a 'scramble' to properly test the story at the last minute. This is unfair to the QA team. If the developers work until the last minute, then the final minute is reserved for testing and packaging, and implementation; which will never happen.

I enforce a 'code complete' step four days before the end of the sprint. Anything not in one of the test environments at that time is considered to be ineligible for inclusion in the sprint deliverables. This means that the developers will not demonstrate the story to the Product Owner and must defend why the commitment to complete the story has not been met.

I also enforce Quality by Design, wherein the developer is responsible for incrementally testing and documenting the test steps and results during the development process.

In a perfect world, no incomplete, untested, or partially functional story would be released to production. But the reality is that, in the rush to meet sprint deadlines, shortcuts will be taken at the expense of quality.

The sprint duration is a fixed timeframe, and all groomed stories should complete within that time frame. However, the sprint duration is an artificial construct for guiding and controlling deliverables. If meeting deadlines takes precedence over quality, then the purpose of the Agile methodology is negated. While meeting deadlines is critical, delivering failed functionality for the sake of being able to complete a sprint on time has no value for the business customer.

Quality should never be compromised for a deadline.

While the Agile methodology can:
- Improve productivity
- Reduce project costs
- Provide for greater customer satisfaction
- Improve the motivation of the team members

Agile does not necessarily have a dramatic benefit on quality. Quality is something that has to be worked toward, continuously. Remember that Agile stresses functionality over quality.

Hence, the need for Quality by Design.

Scrum Framework

Due to the need for agility, the scrum framework is very simple. One of the most important components of Agile and scrum is communication and self-management. The team decides how much work they can accomplish during a sprint while the Scrum Master and Product Owner assume many of the functions of a traditional Project Manager.

Gouldenisn #8*: "Never say or write something you will have to apologize for."*

Since requirements change frequently, the team must continually review their efforts to ensure that they are fulfilling the requirements. Remember that scrum is more of an evolutionary development cycle rather than a 'big bang' solution. Requirements are going to change even as stories are being worked.

Ever-changing requirements and definitions of need are the bane of any project development methodology. In many cases, the detailed requirements are unknown by all until the actual time of implementation.

Agile embraces change and readily accommodates it. This may often produce 'last minute' changes in requirements. However, the magnitude of the story should be such that development and testing can readily accommodate those changes. Agile stories focus on small deliverable functions or components that are typically independent of any other story.

Agile does share some common pitfalls with traditional project management methodologies. All too often, the Scrum team will focus on the tools used to manage the sprint rather than execute the sprint. (Novice project managers will spend all of their time working on their project management software and plans while neglecting the project itself.)

Be wary of any tool or process that hinders the Agile development function; inefficient and bureaucratic processes will make Agile and scrum fail horribly.

Again, the basic Agile concepts also apply to scrum:

1. Processes are not as important as the individual team members and their interactions.
2. Tools do **not** take priority over the individual.
3. The team should spend their time producing a working solution rather than convoluted documentation. (However, documentation is required.)
4. Collaborate with the customer rather than contract with them. (By communicating concerns and ideas with the customer, a better result may evolve while avoiding unnecessary delays or failures.)
5. Always be willing to embrace change rather than try to adhere to a documented plan. (Plans change, especially in Agile.)

As was previously mentioned, the scrum team is essentially a self-managed unit which has the ability to define the team goals and select which stories they will commit to completing during the sprint.

There are a few caveats though. This works well in theory, but is entirely different in reality.

It is human nature is to select the path of least resistance and if not managed properly, the team will commit only to the 'fun' and easy stories, leaving the more difficult (and probably) the more valuable stories to languish in the backlog.

The Product Owner needs to prioritize the stories in the backlog before opening them up for team selection. If properly prioritized, the stories important to the customer will be the ones the team selects from. The team must work with the prioritized list of stories provided by the Product Owner.

Once a team member commits to completing a story within a sprint, there is a moral contract between the team and the Product Owner that those committed stories will be completed. If there are mitigating circumstances that would prevent completion of a committed story, the team member must advise the Scrum Master and Product Owner immediately. Once the team commits to a story, the Product Owner may communicate the sprint stories with the business management team, establishing expectations if what the team will provide during the sprint. (Failure to deliver a committed story is a failure.)

Each team member has the right to 'push back' if the workload is excessive or unrealistic. ('Push back' does not imply a right to refuse to work or accept a task, but to communicate with the Scrum Master and Product Owner so that they can decide which story has precedence.) Ultimately, the goal of development is to provide a solution that has value to the customer.

There may be instances where a story is too complex to complete within a single sprint cycle. In such cases, the Product Owner must break the story into more finite components, possibly resulting in multiple subsequent stories.

While the team members perform the development and many of the support functions, the Scrum Master quietly manages and choreographs the efforts and provides assistance wherever possible. In many instances, the Scrum Master may function as an administrative assistant to the team itself.

The Scrum Master needs to be a task master and an assistant. The Scrum Master's role is also the 'gatekeeper' who works to minimize distractions to the team, and the mentor who helps the team better understand how to optimize their performance.

Scrum and working with sprints is essentially a very simple concept, though it is often difficult to execute. Often, the team tends to over-work a solution. <u>Remember to keep things simple, fulfill the acceptance criteria and do not gold-plate</u>.

Being Agile and working within a scrum requires a mental shift from traditional development methodologies. Sometimes developers experience difficulties making this transition. They will often fall back into old monolithic habits.

Many developers are unaccustomed to working at the frenetic pace of Agile, and may procrastinate. This is where the daily stand-up comes into play. If the Scrum Master or Product Owner sense that the developer is stalling, then there is a need for a discussion with that developer.

The Backlog

The backlog is merely the queue of 'project' requests made by the Product Owner and other stakeholders. Requests are entered in the form of user stories that follow a specific format, as seen below.

The backlog is a constantly changing repository or document that adjusts to the changing needs of the business and the activities of the Scrum Team.

Each story in the Product Backlog must always provide value to the business. There should never be low-level tasks or action items entered into the backlog. Value added stories may not be directly visible to the user and could include back-end processes that improve the quantity or quality of data being used by the business. There is also value in research and infrastructure enhancements. However, the value may not be readily apparent to the business leaders.

With that in mind, it is incumbent upon the Product Owner to ensure that there are always stories with apparent and tangible value in each sprint. Anyone can make entries into the backlog, but only the Product Owner can assign priorities. These priorities are based upon the needs of the business, not the needs of the developers.

The Product Owner must assign a priority to each story on the Backlog and monitor the backlog frequently to ensure proper management of the request queue.

Typically, prior to each sprint, the team will meet with the Product Owner to review the prioritized stories and determine what stories can be completed within the next sprint.

The team 'negotiates' with the Product Owner to balance their capabilities with the needs of the business. As the negotiation progresses, the stories are added to specific sprints.

When a backlog story is moved into an active sprint or imminent sprint, then a greater level of detail should be provided by breaking the story down into discreet tasks and functions.

Trying to define tasks for every story in the backlog could be a waste of time because many of the stories may be removed from the backlog at a future time as the business needs change.

While it is possible to plan ahead for multiple sprints, in most dynamic environments, this is an exercise in futility. The ever-changing nature of the stories and the ebb and flow of business demands make future sprints obsolete as soon as they are planned. (It is best to plan one sprint at a time, and have the planning for the next sprint in progress.)

If the Business demands planning for multiple 'forward-looking' sprints, all parties must understand that those sprints are tentative and subject to dramatic change, depending on the needs of the business. 'Forward-looking' sprints should NEVER be considered a commitment. The volatility of forward-looking sprints MUST be emphasized to the business management team.

Everything in the backlog should be prioritized by the Product Owner and understood by the Scrum team. This prioritization can be based on the needs of the business along with the level of effort, in terms of time or points. Typically, the most important stories are prioritized and moved to the top of the list by means of a 'Critical – High – Medium – Low' rating scale. Anything listed as 'Critical' is at the top of the list.

Once the sprint contents are finalized, each story can be numerically prioritized by developer so that there is a clear understanding by all parties what is the top priority of each developer.

Depending on the size of the backlog, it can be monitored electronically by a commercial application, using spreadsheets, or a white board with notes taped to it. What is used depends on the comfort level and budget of the business.

If a tool is used to manage the backlog, the Product Owner must take steps to ensure that only a select few can alter the backlog. To do otherwise will result in chaos as people randomly move stories around.

Sprint Storyboard

Pending / Backlog	Development	Code Review	Systems Integration	Customer Acceptance	Production
Story #1	Story #4	Story #6	Story #7	Story #9	Story #11
Story #2	Story #5		Story #8	Story #10	Story #12
Story #3					Story #13

Sprints

A sprint is merely a specific period of time during which work is performed. The duration of a sprint is fixed within an organization and cannot be adjusted without approval of the business.

Some teams try to do everything in a sprint. They tend to develop until close to the end of the sprint, and then begin testing. This is a poor practice.

Ideally, as each developer completes a story, it should be team tested, code reviewed, and then turned over to the QA team for testing. That way the testing will progress while development continues.

Scrum teams are self-organized and essentially self-managed. Where possible the team plans for and resolves issues, escalating to the Product Owner when necessary.

Typically, team plans and schedules are available to the public and the stakeholders. They are normally visible at the highest levels of the business. These plans and statuses are, by their nature, very dynamic and constantly changing. This is to be expected.

The Sprint Cycle

The sprint cycle is a pre-defined series of events that are performed in a specific sequence.

The Sprint encompasses all of the development functions: design, development, testing, and implementation. Along with that, there is constant communication among the team members, either formally through sprint events like the daily stand-up meeting, or informally through the course of the development effort.

The Sprint Cycle

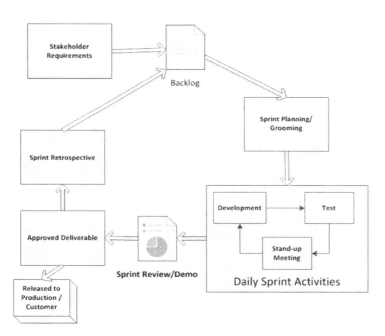

A new sprint will start with two planning meetings: a grooming session (often called a What meeting) and a more technical meeting to determine the complexity and level of effort required for each story (sometimes called the How meeting). Together, these two meeting make up what is called the Sprint Planning Meeting.

In the first meeting, the team, along with the Product Owner determine what stories will be included in the sprint. It is not uncommon for more stories to be selected than can be completed within the Sprint cycle.

Prior to the first Sprint grooming (What) meeting, the Product Owner must complete several tasks:

- A sprint goal must be defined. This is a brief description of the objective of the sprint
- If there is an underlying goal or theme for the sprint, the Product Owner will identify and prioritize stories in the backlog that fit that goal.
- Working with the Scrum Master, the Product Owner may break the stories down into smaller stories (research, demonstration, beta test, etc.) that can be completed within a single sprint.
- Preliminary estimates can be developed by the Product Owner, based upon the business understanding of the level of complexity. (This is important so that the Product Owner is not entirely dependent upon developer estimations, which are typically poor.)
  - Developers will over-estimate, 'padding' their time to ensure they minimize pressure.
  - Sometimes developers will provide an estimate based on what they think the Product Owner 'wants to hear', resulting is grossly under-estimated level of effort for the tasks.
- The Product Owner will work with the Scrum Master to determine team capacity for the sprint. (Vacations and other assignments must be taken into consideration.

After the first meeting, the team should evaluate the stories for complexity. A level of complexity must be assigned to each story. There are a lot of ways to determine complexity. This determination should not be an estimate of time required, that is a separate metric.

Complexity is a measure of how difficult the story may be and is completely independent of the level of effort, which is normally expressed as a time value.

Most commonly, complexity is expressed as elements of a Fibonacci sequence (0, 1, 2, 3, 5, 8, 13, 21, 34, 55, 89, etc.) Each number is the sum of the two numbers preceding it in the sequence ($1+2 = 3$, $2+3 = 5$, etc.) The higher the number, the more complex the story. Typically, the Product Owner is not involved in the estimation of complexity.

Some organizations use a deck of special cards with the Fibonacci numbers on each card and the each member of the team 'throws' a card with their estimation of the level of complexity for each story, based on their individual understanding of the story and what it entails.

Typically, the high and low outliers are discarded unless there is a strong justification. In most cases, the number that occurs most often, or the mode is used to represent the complexity.

At this point, the developers should work up an Input-Process-Output (IPO) chart for each story. If the developer is unable to provide an IPO chart, then there is lack of understanding, or additional clarification is required.

The developer should be able to define the inputs required for the story. This may include database tables, server connections, web services, or other source of data. For the purpose of the IPO chart, field definitions are not necessary; possibly just a reference to a table definition document is all that is needed. If the developer cannot readily identify the input sources

As with the input component, the developer should be able to identify the processes required to complete the story. These should be listed in clear concise order that anyone can review.

Finally, the output should be defined. This may be a textual explanation of what the developer understands is desired, though a screen print or graphical 'mock-up' is better.

Once these three design components are complete, the developer can work with the Product Owner to review them and adjust as necessary.

Story ID:
Title:

Narrative:

Input

Process

Output

Product Owner approval:

The IPO chart allows each story to identify the three critical components: inputs, processes, and outputs. If any of the three components cannot be determined, then the Product Owner must help provide this information, or the story must be returned to the Backlog.

The IPO chart facilitates identifying specific tasks and dependencies on other teams.

Armed with a completed IPO chart, each developer can more readily determine the complexity and the effort required to complete the story.

The Product Owner should review each IPO and confirm that the data sources are correct and that the processing will produce the outputs expected by the business.

Once the Product Owner has approved the IPO, then the developers can consider the story to be legitimate, and eligible to begin work.

Without an IPO, the developer is often left to 'guess' what the outputs should be and how to achieve that result. This can result in a lot of rework being passed into subsequent sprints to make the results of the story match the expectations of the business. Obviously, this will cause the following sprints to fail.

Once the IPO is validated, the How meeting can progress quickly because the developers are not 'guessing' what the goal is. They have performed enough analysis to know what data sources are needed, what type of processing is required, and how the output is to be presented. They can make realistic estimates based on research rather than assumptions. (Too often, complexity estimates are approached with little or no sense of urgency.)

During the course of the sprint, the team keeps each other informed of any issues or progress made. If someone needs to make structural or procedural changes that may affect other team members, the notification and discussion occurs immediately, rather than waiting for a meeting.

The Scrum Master should be thoroughly engaged with the team and its activities, assisting where possible and urging when necessary. Being a coach and assistant is a difficult role that many find challenging.

During the course of the sprint, there is a brief (fifteen minute) 'stand-up' meeting each day, in which each team member identifies what they accomplished the previous day, what their goals are for the next day, and any impediments or obstacles they may have.

The Scrum Master should take ownership of resolving any impediments; though this may also be assumed by a team member, the Product Owner, or a member of the Business Management team.

The Scrum Master must ensure that the team members provide legitimate information in the stand-up. 'Pass' is not an acceptable response (this means they did nothing the previous day and plan on doing nothing the next day). Encourage the team members to not provide the same responses each day; this could be an indication that nothing is being done, or that the team member is overworked.

Near the end of the sprint, there should be two more meetings. The first is a demonstration to the Product Owner where each story is evaluated for completeness and correctness, garnering Product Owner approval to move it to production.

The second meeting is a sprint release meeting wherein each story is presented to the implementation teams; providing a 'heads up' of what is going into production and when the business expects it to be implemented. During this meeting, specific implementers may be assigned or additional information may be requested from the team. This meeting facilitates the overall effectiveness of the sprint by establishing a partnership relationship with the teams that will actually install or implement the sprint stories.

After the sprint has been moved into production, the team should review their stories functioning in the production environment to ensure that they function as intended. This allows to team to proactively identify any defects before the customers identify them. (The developer owns the story, and code, from inception to retirement.) Each day, the developer should access the Production system and ensure that no new issues or defects have been interjected into their processes. While regression testing should eliminate issues like this, it is not uncommon for new code to break a production application.

Finally, the Scrum Master should sponsor a Retrospective meeting to review what went well during the sprint and what did not. Any lessons learned should be identified and documented for use in future sprints.

User Story

A user story consists of a high-level description of the requirements, the user acceptance criteria, notes, points, and estimated task duration. Typically, this is created by the Product Owner, though the developers or Scrum Master may be approached for Subject Matter Expert (SME) knowledge.

Again, be aware that the points are a reflection of the complexity of the story and is independent of the estimated time to complete.

The story description is very high-level narrative and follows a set structure. The advantage to this format is that it provides a structured presentation of the high-level requirements. The disadvantage is that the description is often very ambiguous and poorly suited for detailed analysis of the work required to accomplish it.

Story Description

The story description is an explanation of the requirements in a specific format:

"As a ___(who) , I want _____ (what) so that _____(why).

Typically, additional details may be documented as notes and email communications and should be attached to the story. It is essential that an IPO be developed for each story as soon as possible.

No estimates should be provided or work started without an approved IPO. Lack of an approved IPO will result in failed stories and subsequent rework. If the expectations are not managed at the outset, the expectations will change for the worse.

Acceptance Criteria

The Acceptance criteria are the explanations of the expected end result in a simple standardized format:

Given ___ (Context or event) ___ when___(action)___ then ___(outcome)___.

Remember that the acceptance criteria essentially define the goal of the story. This criteria must be detailed enough to enable the developers to understand the purpose of the story and adequately deliver a viable product to the business.

Test Requirements/Steps

Test Requirements and steps can be simple or complex, depending on the nature of the story. These instructions allow the tester or a user to validate that the deliverable actually accomplishes what is expected.

Be wary of being too precise in defining the test steps, this may restrict testing to a miniscule 'workable' solution that will not work when in production.

The test steps should be detailed enough to allow the tester to develop a test plan and related scripts, but not so detailed that the testing becomes myopic.

Typically, test results are included with the story as it is promoted into the Production environment as documentation for compliance reporting.

Definition of Ready

The definition of 'ready' clarifies when a story is adequately prepared for being groomed into a sprint. There are some important and (sometimes) obvious criteria to be considered.

The value to the business must be clearly articulated. If there is no clearly defined business value, then the story should not be worked.

The story must be independent of other stories, negotiable, valuable, estimable, small enough to complete in a sprint, and testable. If there are complex dependencies, has no value, is too large, or cannot be tested, then it is not a legitimate story.

The acceptance criteria must clearly describe all of the features of the story. Be wary of programmer tendencies to 'gold plate' by adding unrequested features or fixes; this will consume unnecessary hours and inject the potential for undocumented code failures.

A story must be small enough to complete in a single sprint. If the story is too large, then it must be broken down into smaller stories. No story should ever span multiple sprints.

The story must name the Product Owner(s), the Story Owner(s), and have points assigned. If there is no Product Owner, Story Owner, or estimate of points, then the story cannot be worked because it is inadequately defined.

Each story must include tasks and their associated hours. Again, a story with no tasks or time assigned cannot be worked due to improper definition. (It is impossible to do a job if the job requirements are unknown.)

There should be no external dependencies that could prevent the story from being completed within the sprint. If there are external dependencies, then the story should be postponed to a later sprint, after that dependency has been resolved.

Definition of Done

As above, the Definition of 'Done' (DoD) is determined by the team, working in conjunction with the Product Owner, who represents the business, and the Scrum Master.

Typically, the definition of done will have a functionality and a quality component. However, remember that much of the focus of young Scrum teams is focused on functionality over quality.

The definition of done may vary through levels of the Scrum effort. There may be a code complete DoD, a testing DoD, and a post-production DoD.

What a developer calls done may merely mean that it is ready to be tested. When a sprint is released into Production, what the user sees as a Definition of Done may be something entirely different from what was delivered. That is why it is important to demonstrate the Sprint package to the Product Owner so that the entire Scrum team agrees that what is being delivered is what was requested, and is documented in the IPO.

When the code is produced that resolves all tasks, or 'to do' items for the story, then the code can be closed.

The code should be well-commented and checked into and compared with previous versions that are in the source control repository.

It is common practice to have a peer 'code review', though it may be wise to expand this audience to include Database Administrators (DBA), Quality Assurance, Enterprise Architects, Operations, and Management. This will provide a more comprehensive review of the code. This will minimize unexpected surprises when the code is scheduled for implementation.

The code or package must compile/build without errors. If there are errors, then the code is not complete.

All test scripts must execute, pass, and be closed.

Once all of the acceptance criteria have been met, then the story is to be considered complete.

Any changes must be implemented documented and communicated to all interested parties. It does no good to implement changes without advising others. In the event that the application functions differently or has errors, the stakeholder must be made aware of any changes that are implemented.

Finally, all hours for the tasks and stories must be set to zero. If the work is completed, there should be no residual hours remaining on the story.

Scrum Events

Scrum events are specific meetings that must occur in a pre-determined order. They include: Planning meetings, daily stand-up meetings, Pre-release demonstration meetings, release meetings, and the retrospective meeting.

The ideal behind scrum meetings is that they will be well-organized and orchestrated, and to the point. The purpose is to inform and organize instead of filling time. Each meeting event has a specific purpose and goal.

Sprint Grooming Session

The first Scrum event is the Grooming session. During the grooming session, the Product Owner presents the prioritized backlog items in descending order by priority. If the backlog is large, the presentation may be limited to a limited subset, based on the Product Owner's priority.

During this meeting, the team is encouraged and expected to ask questions and get clarification of the requirements for each story in sequence and to identify resources, capacity, skills and knowledge necessary to fulfill the story.

By keeping an eye on team member workload and capacity, the Scrum Master can determine when the sprint is full. At that point, the meeting should be called into a summary phase where the Scrum Master and Product Owner can summarize the goals of the sprint, and the stories expected to be included.

However, it is not uncommon for the business and Product Owner to decide that priorities have changed and that a new story needs to be added to the current sprint. When this happens, it is time for the Scrum Master and the team to negotiate with the Product Owner to determine how to handle the new story.

An additional story may take precedence over an existing story, resulting in one or more stories from the sprint being moved to the backlog. There will also be instances where an existing, lower priority story suddenly escalates to the top priority. This also requires negotiation and rearranging of the sprint, and determining what stories need to move to the next sprint or to the Backlog.

If that is not acceptable to the Product Owner, then it may be necessary to approve overtime in order to fulfill the needs of the business.

I prefer that overtime be avoided so that there is reduced risk of burning out developer resources. That being said, there are legitimate emergencies that require extra effort to complete new tasks that cannot be negotiated. Once a developer agrees to complete a story by the end of the sprint, that commitment must be honored, even if it requires extra hours.

Be aware that no one can work at 100% capacity. At best, no team member should be allocated more than 70%. This allows for distractions such as phone calls, Subject Matter Expert (SME) conversations, meetings, and Scrum Events. This means that in a standard forty hour week, the developer should only have twenty-eight hours of productive time tow work on stories.

Once the sprint has been filled with the acceptable number of stories and all team members have work allocated to them, points and durations are assigned to each story by the person working on them. These numbers are used for the Sprint burn down and velocity metrics.

Once committed, the Sprint is published and each team member is responsible for completing the committed stories, on time and with proper attention to quality. Remember that extra time may need to be expended to complete the committed stories and the developer should self-manage that extra time, while notifying the Scrum Master and Product Owner that more time is being devoted to the story than previously planned.

Burn down refers to the total number of points allocated for the sprint. As stories are worked, the hours assigned to each task must be decremented. When the task is marked complete, the points assigned to it will be decremented as well, providing some indication of the velocity of the team during the sprint.

The Burn Down Chart

The burn down chart is a fundamental tool of the Scrum Master to track sprint progress. It is a time-based report that compares projected effort with daily actuals. It allows management to track the expected sprint performance against reality. This is a valuable metric for the Scrum Master to ensure that the team is working effectively.

With an established team having a stabilized burn down and velocity rate, the backlog can be evaluated to determine capacity and how many sprints are required to work the entire backlog. Of course, this estimate would be contingent upon having a stable backlog, which is highly unlikely.

The burn down report, or chart, reflects completed stories, in terms of points over the life of the sprint. Ideally, there will be a continuous decline in points and hours as each developer consumes time working on a story. If there are upward spikes in the burn down chart, this is indicative of added stories, or a necessary re-estimation of the level of effort.

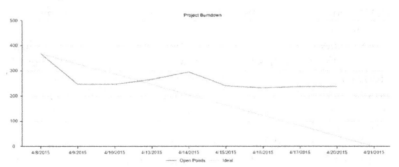

Simple Burn Down Chart

Sprint Velocity

Velocity represents the progress of the team against the stories in the sprint. The only time points are counted in the velocity is when the story is actually completed; there is no credit for partial work. It is either done or not done. If the story is moved to a subsequent sprint, the remaining points are moved with it and contribute to the velocity for that new sprint.

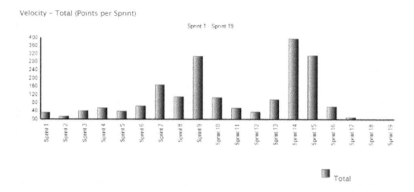

Velocity - Total (Points per Sprint)

Some Scrum Masters prefer to write the stories on cards or paper and post then on a whiteboard for visual tracking of progress. There are also software packages that can automate this tracking process and facilitate reporting. This can also be done with Excel or Visio. What tool is used is of little importance, the management of the sprint is the most important factor.

Typically, there will be columns for None, Design, Development, Code Review, System Integration Testing (SIT), Customer Acceptance Testing (CAT), Ready for PROD (Beta), Production, and Post-PROD.

Note that depending upon the organization, there may be multiple layers of test environments. Depending upon the needs of the business, there may be very specific types and levels of testing and validation that occurs within each environment.

When the sprint is finished, the Scrum Master adds the number of points of completed and delivered stories. (This is based on points and not time.) The total number of completed points for each sprint is the team's velocity for that sprint.

As more sprints are completed, the average velocity is determined by adding all of the completed points for all sprints and dividing by the number of sprints. This average provides a 'smoothed' velocity indicator that is a better measure of the scrum team's actual capability.

Armed with the average velocity, the team can comfortably commit to a specific number of story points for each subsequent sprint. Knowing the average velocity for each scrum team enables the Scrum Master to effectively gauge the capacity and capabilities of the team and provide better control of the sprint.

Sprint Storyboard					
Pending / Backlog	Development	Code Review	Systems Integration	Customer Acceptance	Production
Story #1	Story #4	Story #6	Story #7	Story #9	Story #11
Story #2	Story #5		Story #8	Story #10	Story #12
Story #3					Story #13

Daily-Stand Up Meeting

Each day, there should be a short meeting, not to exceed fifteen minutes, during which the team gathers around a common area and stands up to report their status. The content and reporting style of these daily meetings is consistent and adheres to a defined format.

Some Scrum Masters prefer a morning Stand Up meeting while others prefer one at the end of the day. There are benefits and disadvantages for each. A morning stand up gives time during the day to correct any issues and address impediments. Conversely, by having the stand up at the end of the day, work can be initiated overnight to resolve issues and impediments.

However, once a time has been determined, it must be adhered to. Tardiness should not be tolerated.

During the stand-up the team members follow a simple format of "What I Did yesterday, what I will do today/tomorrow, and what are my impediments." This should not be in depth or highly technical, but should be comprehensive enough to communicate any changes that might impact the other team members, along with any impediments that management or other team members need to resolve.

If there are changes to database structures or indexes, or database connectivity, this must be communicated to all members of the team.

If there is a need for more technical discussions, then 'break-out discussions may be held after the Scrum Master closes the stand-up meeting. <u>Do not let team members hijack the meeting to discuss topics not directly related to Sprint performance</u>.

After each stand-up meeting, the Scrum Master will update the Sprint board (or software) and burn down any hours as necessary.

Make sure that the stand-up meeting is a 'safe' venue where the team can communicate freely without fear of being chastised or punished. The goal is open communications and any punitive actions will quickly suppress the spirit of open communication.

This is not a forum to discuss issues with the team member, or for the team member to voice displeasure or a difference of opinion. Those discussions are better served in a separate meeting not involving the entire team.

Sprint Review Meeting

Prior to the final day of the Sprint, the Scrum Master and the team prepare for a demonstration of the completed stories for the Product Owner(s). The Product Owner must approve each story and confirm that it meets all of his/her requirements and expectations. Any changes or suggestions not specified in the acceptance criteria must be considered as an 'enhancement' story for the next sprint. It is unfair for the Product Owner to inject a new requirement after the story has been groomed and the agreed upon work has been completed.

This meeting should be informal and essentially just a 'hands on' demonstration. Slide shows and extensive documentation is not necessary or desired. Since the Scrum Master is closely engaged with the development process, preparation for this meeting should require minimal effort.

Only completed stories are presented. If there are stories that could not be completed, the Scrum Master must be prepared to explain why.

There are legitimate reasons for stories to be incomplete during a sprint. Developers are human and their estimating skills may be somewhat lacking. Typically, developers will make two significant errors in their estimation process:

1 – They will provide an estimate that is what they think the Product Owner wants to hear.

2 – They will over-estimate to allow for 'surprises'.

Again, the Scrum Master must be aware that it is impossible for anyone to work at 100% of capacity. There are always constant interruptions that 'nibble away' at available time. This is different for every person, and is called the Work Interruption Factor.

Never allocate a person at 100%. I recommend no more than 70%. Some of the team, especially the Subject Matter Experts (SMEs) may have a much lower time allocation availability due to their support for other team members.

If you have a team member assigned more than 70%, there is a high probability for failure, because that person will most likely be overworked.

After the Product Owner has approved the stories for implementation into Production, the Scrum Master should schedule a meeting with the implementers so that they can be apprised of the changes and impacts offered by the new stories. This helps avoid unpleasant surprises to the implementers and allows them to manage their own resource planning.

In many cases, new stories will be identified during this meeting that the Product Owner can prioritize and add to the backlog for future sprints.

Note: I prefer to hold a preliminary sprint review meeting on what I call the 'Code Complete' day, which is typically a week before the end of the sprint and prior to official testing. This gives the developers a chance to demonstrate the story and confirm with the Product Owner that what they have developed truly meets the needs of the business.

This provides an opportunity for rework or adjusting the sprint if there is a huge discrepancy between what has been developed and what is expected. This also avoids the problem of demonstrating an improper product at the last minute, giving the Product Owner the ability to better manage the expectations of the stakeholders.

The day after 'Code Complete' and after the Product Owner has reviewed and approved story results, I schedule a formal meeting with the implementation teams and allow the developers to briefly explain their stories and installation scripts and packages, highlighting any unique or extraordinary requirements. At this meeting, the implementers freely ask questions and offer advice for improving the installation processes.

Some key points of interest that need to be provided include:

- Does any application system need to be shut down prior to implementation?
- Do the stories need to be implemented in a specific order?
- What are the dependencies?
- Do supporting jobs need to be shut down and restarted?
- How long should each implementation step take and who to contact?

Sprint Retrospective Meeting

At the end of the sprint and after the stories have been implemented, the Scrum Master should have a Sprint Retrospective Meeting scheduled with all of the stakeholders, and most specifically, the Product Owner. The implementers must be included in this meeting.

During this meeting, what was done wrong, what was done well, and areas of improvement should be openly discussed. This is not a forum for applying blame or making excuses; it should be an open evaluation of how the entire scrum team performed (remember that the Product Owner is part of the team as well).

This meeting provides a safe, non-confrontational environment for examining how the team performed and how it can improve. This is part of what Agile refers to as 'inspect and adapt', where the team learns from its mistakes and successes.

Remember that the goal of the retrospective meeting is continuous improvement. If the implementation teams experienced problems, then this must be shared with the scrum team so they can correct the problem before the

After the retrospective, the Scrum Master publishes the meeting notes and publishes the release notes so that the user community can be informed about the new features and changes.

The entire team should take these 'lessons learned' to heart and apply them to the next sprint in the spirit of continuous improvement.

If there are procedural or political issues, the Product Owner should work to resolve those issues for future sprints.

Release Notes

The release notes should be a clear, concise, human-readable explanation of the features provided by the sprint. It may be best if a non-technical team member draft the release notes so that technical jargon and obscurities are not used. The audience for the release notes is the general user community, not the developers.

This document provides a quick, high-level overview of the benefits provided by the sprint efforts. It is an opportunity to 'brag' and gain positive public relations for the team.

The release notes provide a very powerful communication tool that allows the user community to see and understand what the development team is delivering during each sprint. Ideally, the team can foster a sense of anticipation among the user community so that they eagerly look to see what new feature has been provided by the developers.

Sprint Close-out

Once the code has been implemented and the stories are closed, the Scrum Master can close the sprint by zeroing the hours and 'burning down' the points.

Any story not completed during the sprint must be revisited with the Product Owner to determine if they will move into the next sprint or be moved to the backlog.

Be wary of the temptation to automatically move unfinished stories into the next sprint. This may result in an excessively full sprint that is impossible to complete, which will start a vicious cycle of failed sprints. The Product Owner must decide what will be included in each sprint.

What Can Go Wrong?

What can go wrong with Agile? Like any concept or tool, anything can go wrong and probably will. As with any tool, you will have to adapt it to meet unique needs as you learn to use it.

Many people feel that they can buy a book on Agile, or attend a seminar or training session and become an Agile expert. This will not be the case.

Note: Reading this book will not make you an Agile expert.

The way to become an Agile expert is to work it and live it. Theoretical Agile concepts will not work, but experiential Agile will work, though each organization may approach Agile differently. The point is that Agile is adaptive and should never be viewed as an inflexible formula.

Remember that if the development team is Agile while the rest of the organization is grounded in a monolithic, process-restrictive environment, the benefits of Agile will not be realized by the business.

It is imperative that Agile be supported at the Executive level and all lower levels of management. Attempting to implement Agile without the backing of the executive management team will result in failure at many levels, including careers.

As mentioned earlier, if the organization retains its monolithic governance and policies and procedures, Agile will fail. Why try to implement an Agile development methodology if the delivery and deployment process is burdensome, bureaucratic, and overly convoluted? No benefits will be realized by the business.

Implementing Agile involves changing the way a business operates internally with respect to projects and development. Agile coaches will attack 'waterfall' methodologies in development, but say nothing about those same methodologies in other areas that may affect the viability of an Agile implementation.

Changing established processes can be one of the greatest challenges to implementing Agile. This is why Executive support is critical; historical, monolithic process must change and adapt to an Agile environment.

Do not expect Agile to work for all projects. Systems that are in 'maintenance mode' are poor candidates for Agile, since they are not as dynamic as a new development or significantly redesigned project. Agile is a great tool for rapid deployment of deliverables, but do not expect it to cure all problems. Many development problems can be traced to organizational or systemic issues and need to be evaluated by the executive team.

Agile will only be as effective as the slowest team in the deployment process, the weak link.

Quality by Design

Overview

There are countless philosophies regarding Quality Assurance and how to achieve 'Zero Defects' in a manufacturing or production environment. Less effort has been expended in defining the quality requirements for a software development environment. While quality standards have been developed for the more traditional environments and industries, corporate Information Services Departments often lag behind.

Borrowing heavily from one of the most regulated industries in the world, American Food and Drugs, we can identify four key metrics and focal points of opportunity to improve the quality of Corporate Information Services efforts. These metrics are:

- **DQ** - **D**esign **Q**uality
- **OQ** - **O**perational **Q**uality
- **PQ** - **P**rocedural **Q**uality
- **IQ** - **I**mplementation **Q**uality

We also use a Quality Scorecard to measure the ongoing quality lifecycle of the project or application. On the scorecard, there is a column for each of the Development Quality metrics above as well as columns for the QA functions and the post-implementation cycle.

Please keep in mind that these first four design quality checkpoints MUST be performed before turning the application over to any formal QA function in order to have any level of relevance.

DQ: Design Quality

As the name implies, this involves designing for quality before the programming even begins. This requires involvement of the user in an iterative process whereby the development team partners with the user community to identify:

- What the user and functional requirements are

- What requests can be technologically achieved.

Normally, this function is performed by the project design team while working closely with Product Owner(s), Business Analysts, and other Subject Matter Experts (SME). This is an iterative process wherein the design of the product and deliverables is refined and agreed upon by all parties.

The process begins after a user request has been received by the Information Services department. Commonly referred to as the fact-finding stage, it involves open discussion and cooperation to clearly identify what the user community requires. It then involves melding those requirements with the Information Services standards and corporate goals that will produce an application or system that functions reliably within the current and future Information Services environment.

Flexibility and adaptability are key criteria during this phase. In this phase, screen and report mock-ups are presented and iteratively modified until all requirements have been achieved, including Information Service design standards.

When a consensus has been reached among the user and developer community, the drafts are signed by the user sponsor and the Information Services representative and the project scope document can be drafted. The process is then documented, including project scope, process flow, Work Breakdown Structures (WBS). The mock-ups of screen and report layouts have already been approved and signed by the users and sponsors. Note that some of this documentation may be waived in an Agile development environment.

When the documentation package is complete, it is presented to a Design Review committee. The purpose of this committee is not to redesign the application requested and approved by the users, but to ensure that critical aspects of design characteristics have not been overlooked. This ensures that the design has the flexibility to support future needs of the business. This review must adopt a 'forward-looking' attitude and not base its decisions and recommendations on historical perspectives. To do otherwise is to force mediocrity into the application or system.

Any significant changes in the design that are made by the Review Committee must be approved by the user sponsor. These changes should be limited to standardization, flexibility, and utility, and not based on how thing have been done in the past.

Once the Review Committee and the User Sponsor agree to the design, it can be turned over to the development team. At this point, the Design Quality (**DQ**) metric measurements begin. As the development team begins work, there may be design flaws or shortages that come to light as those with more detailed knowledge get involved. Any design changes discovered and suggested by the development team should be recorded on the scorecard by the Scrum Master or QA Lead.

PQ: Procedural Quality

The core theme behind defining Procedural Quality is the enforcement of clearly defined programming standards. Modularity and code re-usability are critical success factors.

This level of quality is incorporated by the developers and their managers. (DQ/PQ/OQ/IQ quality checks are ALL primarily performed by the development team.)

While the definition of the standards is incumbent upon the Information Services Management team, the actual implementation rests in the hands of the developers. There must be management oversight and involvement to ensure that the standards are being followed.

With the implementation of standards and pre-defined common modules, the foundation of every program will be established and the developer can concentrate on the business logic rather than continually spending time developing repetitious routines. The corollary to this is that the basic flow and navigation of every program will work exactly the same, reducing the effort required to test in the QA areas.

As the development team continues work on the product or application, structural flaws may become apparent. Additional modules or programs may be affected that were not identified in earlier stages. These discoveries and observations may require changes to the scope that must be approved by the sponsors, since these changes may impact the Cost and Time Baselines. Procedural Quality (**PQ**) focuses on the individual components that make up the entire application or product.

Any flaws or defects must be recorded on the Quality Scorecard.

OQ: Operational Quality

Operational Quality ensures that the components of the application or system will interact with other functions and applications as the users expect when it is delivered. Typically, this is an iterative process performed by the members of the development team. Any issues requiring correction are coordinated among themselves for resolution. However, the Scrum Master and Product Owner must be informed of any issues, which must be recorded in the Operational Quality (**OQ**) section of the Scorecard. Issues discovered at this stage in the Development Quality cycle could indicate serious design flaws, and should be documented for future efforts.

If any significant changes to the design or functionality of the system or application are identified and recommended by the OQ team, it should be reviewed and approved by the Sponsors, users, and the Review Committee to ensure that the changes will satisfy the needs of the user, adhere to standards, and maintain the flexibility to support future needs of the business. Close attention to the Cost and Time Baselines must be maintained.

IQ: Implementation Quality

The final component of the development quality definition is at the installation level. Normally, this is performed by a team that is responsible for documentation, training, packaging, and installation.

Segregating this group from development and Quality Assurance teams provides a fourth level of quality checking to be applied to the overall development process. It is not uncommon for members of this team to discover problems and issues that were over-looked by the users, developers, and QA team.

By combining the different viewpoints from these distinctive team members, we can provide a closer view of what the actual end-user will see and experience. With some control and monitoring, this provides a final point to eliminate errors and flaws before going through a formal QA process.

The first step in the process is performed by the Scrum Master who must ensure that all documentation is correct and matches the application; that the application actually functions in accordance with the defined functional requirements; and that the supporting turnover documentation will allow other members of the IQ team to perform their assessment and functional responsibilities. Any flaws or omissions discovered by the Project Manager should be recorded on the scorecard in the Implementation Quality (**IQ**) column and returned to the development team to make the necessary corrections.

QA: Quality Assurance

This requires establishing standard test scripts to test each application or system by approved criteria. The acceptance criteria are provided by the Product Owner while the actual test steps and scripts are often provided by the development team.

Often the lower test environments do not contain a full set of up to date test data, so the test teams may need assistance finding valid data to test with.

Typically, testing is an iterative process performed by the members of the Quality Assurance team. Any issues requiring correction are coordinated with the developers for resolution.

If any significant change to the design or functionality of the system or application are identified and recommended by the QA team, it should be reviewed and approved by the Product Owner, users, and the Review Committee to ensure that the change will satisfy the needs of the user, adhere to standards, and maintain the flexibility to support future needs of the business.

The QA team is responsible for fully testing the story or application. This includes regression testing to ensure that the new code does not 'break' any existing code in Production.

In any event, all defects identified by the QA team must be recorded on the Scorecard by the Scrum Master or the QA Lead.

The defects identified by the QA team will illustrate areas of improvement for the design and development teams and areas where they need additional work on their testing procedures.

It is important to note that at the end of the fourth QA cycle, the results ONLY indicate the perception of the level of quality from the standpoint of the development and QA teams. At this point, the user perception is not available.

Post-Implementation Evaluation

We take the stance that the first month after implementation of a project or application; it is still under the auspices of Project

Management and the full ownership of the Project Manager; essentially a warranty period. This provides a better framework to determine our overall project performance. Any defects discovered during this phase must be corrected as quickly as possible since they may adversely affect application performance or the overall perception of the application itself.

It is very common for an application or project to be delivered to the user community, thinking that the resulting product is feature-rich, easy to use, and meets the needs of the user. However, until the time the product is in the hands of the end-users, the development team has absolutely no metric to determine the value of the product to the user community. That is why the Post-Implementation Evaluation is essential.

It is incumbent upon the Scrum Master to track all project or application problems that are experienced by the users during this first four week period. This allows for identification of design flaws or shortfalls as well as providing a mechanism to track the effectiveness of the Quality Assurance and Training & Documentation teams.

By keeping the project 'open' during the first four weeks of implementation, we can gather valuable information to improve future efforts. While this extends the Cost and Time baselines a bit, it should be accounted for in the initial budgeting and scheduling processes.

The Scrum Master should track each problem on a daily or weekly basis, depending upon the duration of the sprint. The completed Project Scorecard with graphic and supporting line items should be a fundamental document used in the sprint retrospective meetings. It is not intended to be a 'punitive' tool, but rather a broad 'how did we really do' versus what we think we did.

The final scorecard can be invaluable in identifying shortages in the quality lifecycle.

In the example, the developers discovered issues after the design approval, and had to go back to the review team and Sponsors to get those design shortages included in the scope.

After turning it over to QA, the four-week QA cycle found relatively few defects before handing it over to the Training, Documentation, and Implementation teams. Upon initial implementation, the number of flaws and problems escalated quickly. This could indicate to the team that better oversight is required on the QA, Training, and Documentation processes.

Finally, this graph clearly indicates the differing viewpoints of the Development and QA teams when contrasted with the views of the end-users. At the end of the QA cycle, the defect count was near zero. During the first week of implementation, the errors escalated to over forty, much higher than any point during the development/testing cycle.

With an unbiased and open dialogue at the Sprint Retrospective meeting, each functional manager may see areas of improvement. Even if the Scrum Master categorizes an error incorrectly, the counts will remain the same, illustrating the overall quality of the project from the viewpoint of the end-user.

Summary

In summary, Designing for Quality requires:

    1. Use of four additional quality metrics beyond the typical Quality Assurance team;

        a. **D**esign **Q**uality –

        b. **O**perational **Q**uality -

        c. **P**rocedural **Q**uality -

        d. **I**mplementation **Q**uality -

    2. Accurately track, categorize, and record every flaw, shortfall, defect, error, and bug.

    3. Use the Quality Scorecard to monitor and report the Project Quality Progress.

    4. Inclusion of the Post Implementation cycle as a Quality metric on all projects.

Closing Thoughts

While Agile provides a powerful tool for refactoring development delivery methodologies within a business, it focuses more on delivering functionality than on quality. This is not to say that Agile deliverables lack quality. It means that Agile teams must be more attentive to quality than they would be in a normal monolithic development process.

To help address the potential shortfall of quality in Agile development processes, I recommend implementing Quality by Design as an integrated process that works with Agile to improve the overall quality of the deliverables to the business.

Agile can also be compromised if bureaucratic processes hinder the rapid deployment of Agile stories. If it takes two weeks to work through implementation processes for a two-week agile sprint, the true delivery cycle is four weeks rather than the anticipated two-week delivery promised to the business by the Agile team.

For Agile to be effective, Executive management must support the process and actively work to encourage organizational change to ensure that processes are in place to accommodate and complement the Agile development methodology.

Again, this book will not make anyone an Agile expert; its intent is to provide enough information to allow one to begin working with Agile and to understand the core Agile concepts.

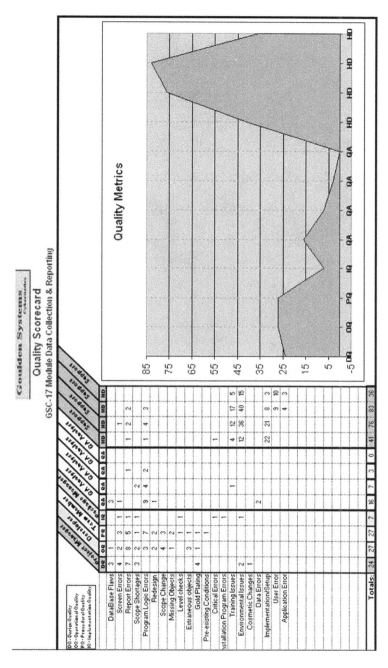

Additional works by Ronald N. Goulden

http://www.rongoulden.com/Literary.htm

Business

Project Management for a Functional World
http://www.amazon.com/dp/1449996590/ Paperback

Learn Excel with the Quality Scorecard
http://www.amazon.com/dp/1450557155/ Paperback
http://www.amazon.com/dp/B0053GKQGY/ Kindle

Learn Excel: Executive Summary & Scope
http://www.amazon.com/dp/1467905356/ Paperback